STUDENT'S NAME

LAST | FIRST | MI

SCHOOL:
TEACHER:
FEMALE ○   MALE ○

BIRTH DATE

MONTH	DAY		YEAR	
Jan ○	⓪	⓪	⓪	⓪
Feb ○	①	①	①	①
Mar ○	②	②	②	②
Apr ○	③	③	③	③
May ○		④	④	④
Jun ○		⑤	⑤	⑤
Jul ○		⑥	⑥	⑥
Aug ○		⑦	⑦	⑦
Sep ○		⑧	⑧	⑧
Oct ○		⑨	⑨	⑨
Nov ○				
Dec ○				

GRADE ② ③ ④ ⑤ ⑥

Higher Scores on Reading Standardized Tests, Grade 3
© Steck-Vaughn Company

(Student name and birth-date bubble grids A–Z)

Unit 1 Pretest

1. Ⓐ Ⓑ Ⓒ Ⓓ   3. Ⓐ Ⓑ Ⓒ Ⓓ   5. Ⓐ Ⓑ Ⓒ Ⓓ   7. Ⓐ Ⓑ Ⓒ Ⓓ
2. Ⓐ Ⓑ Ⓒ Ⓓ   4. Ⓐ Ⓑ Ⓒ Ⓓ   6. Ⓐ Ⓑ Ⓒ Ⓓ   8. Ⓐ Ⓑ Ⓒ Ⓓ

Unit 2 Pretest

1. Ⓐ Ⓑ Ⓒ Ⓓ   4. Ⓐ Ⓑ Ⓒ Ⓓ   7. Ⓐ Ⓑ Ⓒ Ⓓ   10. Ⓐ Ⓑ Ⓒ Ⓓ
2. Ⓐ Ⓑ Ⓒ Ⓓ   5. Ⓐ Ⓑ Ⓒ Ⓓ   8. Ⓐ Ⓑ Ⓒ Ⓓ   11. Ⓐ Ⓑ Ⓒ Ⓓ
3. Ⓐ Ⓑ Ⓒ Ⓓ   6. Ⓐ Ⓑ Ⓒ Ⓓ   9. Ⓐ Ⓑ Ⓒ Ⓓ   12. Ⓐ Ⓑ Ⓒ Ⓓ

Unit 3 Pretest

1. Ⓐ Ⓑ Ⓒ Ⓓ   4. Ⓐ Ⓑ Ⓒ Ⓓ   7. Ⓐ Ⓑ Ⓒ Ⓓ   10. Ⓐ Ⓑ Ⓒ Ⓓ   13. Ⓐ Ⓑ Ⓒ Ⓓ
2. Ⓐ Ⓑ Ⓒ Ⓓ   5. Ⓐ Ⓑ Ⓒ Ⓓ   8. Ⓐ Ⓑ Ⓒ Ⓓ   11. Ⓐ Ⓑ Ⓒ Ⓓ   14. Ⓐ Ⓑ Ⓒ Ⓓ
3. Ⓐ Ⓑ Ⓒ Ⓓ   6. Ⓐ Ⓑ Ⓒ Ⓓ   9. Ⓐ Ⓑ Ⓒ Ⓓ   12. Ⓐ Ⓑ Ⓒ Ⓓ

Unit 1 Posttest

1. Ⓐ Ⓑ Ⓒ Ⓓ   3. Ⓐ Ⓑ Ⓒ Ⓓ   5. Ⓐ Ⓑ Ⓒ Ⓓ   7. Ⓐ Ⓑ Ⓒ Ⓓ
2. Ⓐ Ⓑ Ⓒ Ⓓ   4. Ⓐ Ⓑ Ⓒ Ⓓ   6. Ⓐ Ⓑ Ⓒ Ⓓ   8. Ⓐ Ⓑ Ⓒ Ⓓ

Unit 2 Posttest

1. Ⓐ Ⓑ Ⓒ Ⓓ   4. Ⓐ Ⓑ Ⓒ Ⓓ   7. Ⓐ Ⓑ Ⓒ Ⓓ   10. Ⓐ Ⓑ Ⓒ Ⓓ
2. Ⓐ Ⓑ Ⓒ Ⓓ   5. Ⓐ Ⓑ Ⓒ Ⓓ   8. Ⓐ Ⓑ Ⓒ Ⓓ   11. Ⓐ Ⓑ Ⓒ Ⓓ
3. Ⓐ Ⓑ Ⓒ Ⓓ   6. Ⓐ Ⓑ Ⓒ Ⓓ   9. Ⓐ Ⓑ Ⓒ Ⓓ   12. Ⓐ Ⓑ Ⓒ Ⓓ

Unit 3 Posttest

1. Ⓐ Ⓑ Ⓒ Ⓓ   4. Ⓐ Ⓑ Ⓒ Ⓓ   7. Ⓐ Ⓑ Ⓒ Ⓓ   10. Ⓐ Ⓑ Ⓒ Ⓓ
2. Ⓐ Ⓑ Ⓒ Ⓓ   5. Ⓐ Ⓑ Ⓒ Ⓓ   8. Ⓐ Ⓑ Ⓒ Ⓓ   11. Ⓐ Ⓑ Ⓒ Ⓓ
3. Ⓐ Ⓑ Ⓒ Ⓓ   6. Ⓐ Ⓑ Ⓒ Ⓓ   9. Ⓐ Ⓑ Ⓒ Ⓓ

Lesson 1: Classifying Words

1. Ⓐ Ⓑ Ⓒ Ⓓ	6. Ⓐ Ⓑ Ⓒ Ⓓ	11. Ⓐ Ⓑ Ⓒ Ⓓ	16. Ⓐ Ⓑ Ⓒ Ⓓ	21. Ⓐ Ⓑ Ⓒ Ⓓ
2. Ⓐ Ⓑ Ⓒ Ⓓ	7. Ⓐ Ⓑ Ⓒ Ⓓ	12. Ⓐ Ⓑ Ⓒ Ⓓ	17. Ⓐ Ⓑ Ⓒ Ⓓ	22. Ⓐ Ⓑ Ⓒ Ⓓ
3. Ⓐ Ⓑ Ⓒ Ⓓ	8. Ⓐ Ⓑ Ⓒ Ⓓ	13. Ⓐ Ⓑ Ⓒ Ⓓ	18. Ⓐ Ⓑ Ⓒ Ⓓ	23. Ⓐ Ⓑ Ⓒ Ⓓ
4. Ⓐ Ⓑ Ⓒ Ⓓ	9. Ⓐ Ⓑ Ⓒ Ⓓ	14. Ⓐ Ⓑ Ⓒ Ⓓ	19. Ⓐ Ⓑ Ⓒ Ⓓ	24. Ⓐ Ⓑ Ⓒ Ⓓ
5. Ⓐ Ⓑ Ⓒ Ⓓ	10. Ⓐ Ⓑ Ⓒ Ⓓ	15. Ⓐ Ⓑ Ⓒ Ⓓ	20. Ⓐ Ⓑ Ⓒ Ⓓ	

Lesson 2: Using Synonyms

1. Ⓐ Ⓑ Ⓒ Ⓓ	4. Ⓐ Ⓑ Ⓒ Ⓓ	7. Ⓐ Ⓑ Ⓒ Ⓓ	10. Ⓐ Ⓑ Ⓒ Ⓓ	13. Ⓐ Ⓑ Ⓒ Ⓓ
2. Ⓐ Ⓑ Ⓒ Ⓓ	5. Ⓐ Ⓑ Ⓒ Ⓓ	8. Ⓐ Ⓑ Ⓒ Ⓓ	11. Ⓐ Ⓑ Ⓒ Ⓓ	14. Ⓐ Ⓑ Ⓒ Ⓓ
3. Ⓐ Ⓑ Ⓒ Ⓓ	6. Ⓐ Ⓑ Ⓒ Ⓓ	9. Ⓐ Ⓑ Ⓒ Ⓓ	12. Ⓐ Ⓑ Ⓒ Ⓓ	

Lesson 3: Finding Antonyms

1. Ⓐ Ⓑ Ⓒ Ⓓ	4. Ⓐ Ⓑ Ⓒ Ⓓ	7. Ⓐ Ⓑ Ⓒ Ⓓ	10. Ⓐ Ⓑ Ⓒ Ⓓ
2. Ⓐ Ⓑ Ⓒ Ⓓ	5. Ⓐ Ⓑ Ⓒ Ⓓ	8. Ⓐ Ⓑ Ⓒ Ⓓ	11. Ⓐ Ⓑ Ⓒ Ⓓ
3. Ⓐ Ⓑ Ⓒ Ⓓ	6. Ⓐ Ⓑ Ⓒ Ⓓ	9. Ⓐ Ⓑ Ⓒ Ⓓ	12. Ⓐ Ⓑ Ⓒ Ⓓ

Lesson 4: Understanding Words with More Than One Meaning

1. Ⓐ Ⓑ Ⓒ Ⓓ	4. Ⓐ Ⓑ Ⓒ Ⓓ	7. Ⓐ Ⓑ Ⓒ Ⓓ	10. Ⓐ Ⓑ Ⓒ Ⓓ	13. Ⓐ Ⓑ Ⓒ Ⓓ
2. Ⓐ Ⓑ Ⓒ Ⓓ	5. Ⓐ Ⓑ Ⓒ Ⓓ	8. Ⓐ Ⓑ Ⓒ Ⓓ	11. Ⓐ Ⓑ Ⓒ Ⓓ	
3. Ⓐ Ⓑ Ⓒ Ⓓ	6. Ⓐ Ⓑ Ⓒ Ⓓ	9. Ⓐ Ⓑ Ⓒ Ⓓ	12. Ⓐ Ⓑ Ⓒ Ⓓ	

Lesson 5: Choosing Words with More Than One Meaning

1. Ⓐ Ⓑ Ⓒ Ⓓ	3. Ⓐ Ⓑ Ⓒ Ⓓ	5. Ⓐ Ⓑ Ⓒ Ⓓ
2. Ⓐ Ⓑ Ⓒ Ⓓ	4. Ⓐ Ⓑ Ⓒ Ⓓ	6. Ⓐ Ⓑ Ⓒ Ⓓ

Lesson 6: Using Context Clues

1. Ⓐ Ⓑ Ⓒ Ⓓ	4. Ⓐ Ⓑ Ⓒ Ⓓ	7. Ⓐ Ⓑ Ⓒ Ⓓ	10. Ⓐ Ⓑ Ⓒ Ⓓ
2. Ⓐ Ⓑ Ⓒ Ⓓ	5. Ⓐ Ⓑ Ⓒ Ⓓ	8. Ⓐ Ⓑ Ⓒ Ⓓ	11. Ⓐ Ⓑ Ⓒ Ⓓ
3. Ⓐ Ⓑ Ⓒ Ⓓ	6. Ⓐ Ⓑ Ⓒ Ⓓ	9. Ⓐ Ⓑ Ⓒ Ⓓ	12. Ⓐ Ⓑ Ⓒ Ⓓ

Lesson 7: Arranging Sentences in Correct Order

1. Ⓐ Ⓑ Ⓒ Ⓓ	4. Ⓐ Ⓑ Ⓒ Ⓓ	7. Ⓐ Ⓑ Ⓒ Ⓓ	10. Ⓐ Ⓑ Ⓒ Ⓓ
2. Ⓐ Ⓑ Ⓒ Ⓓ	5. Ⓐ Ⓑ Ⓒ Ⓓ	8. Ⓐ Ⓑ Ⓒ Ⓓ	11. Ⓐ Ⓑ Ⓒ Ⓓ
3. Ⓐ Ⓑ Ⓒ Ⓓ	6. Ⓐ Ⓑ Ⓒ Ⓓ	9. Ⓐ Ⓑ Ⓒ Ⓓ	

Lesson 8: Choosing Titles

1. Ⓐ Ⓑ Ⓒ Ⓓ	3. Ⓐ Ⓑ Ⓒ Ⓓ	5. Ⓐ Ⓑ Ⓒ Ⓓ
2. Ⓐ Ⓑ Ⓒ Ⓓ	4. Ⓐ Ⓑ Ⓒ Ⓓ	6. Ⓐ Ⓑ Ⓒ Ⓓ

Lesson 9: Reading Stories

1. Ⓐ Ⓑ Ⓒ Ⓓ	5. Ⓐ Ⓑ Ⓒ Ⓓ	9. Ⓐ Ⓑ Ⓒ Ⓓ	13. Ⓐ Ⓑ Ⓒ Ⓓ
2. Ⓐ Ⓑ Ⓒ Ⓓ	6. Ⓐ Ⓑ Ⓒ Ⓓ	10. Ⓐ Ⓑ Ⓒ Ⓓ	14. Ⓐ Ⓑ Ⓒ Ⓓ
3. Ⓐ Ⓑ Ⓒ Ⓓ	7. Ⓐ Ⓑ Ⓒ Ⓓ	11. Ⓐ Ⓑ Ⓒ Ⓓ	15. Ⓐ Ⓑ Ⓒ Ⓓ
4. Ⓐ Ⓑ Ⓒ Ⓓ	8. Ⓐ Ⓑ Ⓒ Ⓓ	12. Ⓐ Ⓑ Ⓒ Ⓓ	16. Ⓐ Ⓑ Ⓒ Ⓓ

Lesson 10: Reading Longer Stories

1. Ⓐ Ⓑ Ⓒ Ⓓ	5. Ⓐ Ⓑ Ⓒ Ⓓ	9. Ⓐ Ⓑ Ⓒ Ⓓ	13. Ⓐ Ⓑ Ⓒ Ⓓ	17. Ⓐ Ⓑ Ⓒ Ⓓ
2. Ⓐ Ⓑ Ⓒ Ⓓ	6. Ⓐ Ⓑ Ⓒ Ⓓ	10. Ⓐ Ⓑ Ⓒ Ⓓ	14. Ⓐ Ⓑ Ⓒ Ⓓ	
3. Ⓐ Ⓑ Ⓒ Ⓓ	7. Ⓐ Ⓑ Ⓒ Ⓓ	11. Ⓐ Ⓑ Ⓒ Ⓓ	15. Ⓐ Ⓑ Ⓒ Ⓓ	
4. Ⓐ Ⓑ Ⓒ Ⓓ	8. Ⓐ Ⓑ Ⓒ Ⓓ	12. Ⓐ Ⓑ Ⓒ Ⓓ	16. Ⓐ Ⓑ Ⓒ Ⓓ	

Lesson 11: Reading Poems

1. Ⓐ Ⓑ Ⓒ Ⓓ	3. Ⓐ Ⓑ Ⓒ Ⓓ	5. Ⓐ Ⓑ Ⓒ Ⓓ
2. Ⓐ Ⓑ Ⓒ Ⓓ	4. Ⓐ Ⓑ Ⓒ Ⓓ	6. Ⓐ Ⓑ Ⓒ Ⓓ

Name _____ Date _____

Unit 1 Pretest

Your score: _____

⏱ **You have 10 minutes to complete the Unit 1 test.**

Lesson 1: Classifying Words

Directions Darken the circle by the word that <u>does not</u> belong with the other words in the group.

1. Ⓐ corn
   Ⓑ bread
   Ⓒ peas
   Ⓓ tomatoes

2. Ⓐ kite
   Ⓑ ball
   Ⓒ bat
   Ⓓ house

3. Ⓐ Sun
   Ⓑ Moon
   Ⓒ stars
   Ⓓ ocean

4. Ⓐ street
   Ⓑ summer
   Ⓒ spring
   Ⓓ winter

Lesson 2: Using Synonyms

Directions Darken the circle by the word that has the <u>same</u> or <u>almost the same</u> meaning as the underlined word.

5. <u>close</u> the door
   Ⓐ open
   Ⓑ touch
   Ⓒ shut
   Ⓓ see

6. move <u>rapidly</u>
   Ⓐ stiffly
   Ⓑ swiftly
   Ⓒ slowly
   Ⓓ freely

Lesson 3: Finding Antonyms

Directions Darken the circle by the word that means the <u>opposite</u> of the underlined word.

7. a <u>straight</u> line
   Ⓐ sharp
   Ⓑ dotted
   Ⓒ crooked
   Ⓓ short

8. <u>careful</u> work
   Ⓐ good
   Ⓑ interesting
   Ⓒ hard
   Ⓓ careless

STOP

Higher Scores on Reading Standardized Tests 3, SV 2057-5

Name _____ Date _____

Unit 2 Pretest

⏱ **You have 15 minutes to complete the Unit 2 test.**

Lesson 4: Understanding Words with More Than One Meaning.

Directions Darken the circle by the word that has both underlined meanings.

1. <u>a measurement</u>
    <u>a place to play</u>
    - Ⓐ inch
    - Ⓑ foot
    - Ⓒ yard
    - Ⓓ park

2. <u>a kind of porch</u>
    <u>a pack of cards</u>
    - Ⓐ patio
    - Ⓑ set
    - Ⓒ veranda
    - Ⓓ deck

3. <u>sharp part of a knife</u>
    <u>one piece of grass</u>
    - Ⓐ blade
    - Ⓑ point
    - Ⓒ leaf
    - Ⓓ handle

4. <u>record songs</u>
    <u>fasten with a sticky strip</u>
    - Ⓐ tie
    - Ⓑ rope
    - Ⓒ sing
    - Ⓓ tape

Lesson 5: Choosing Words With More Than One Meaning

Directions Darken the circle by the word with a meaning that fits both of the sentences.

5. Please _____ me that book.
    I hurt my _____ with the scissors.
    - Ⓐ read
    - Ⓑ sell
    - Ⓒ hand
    - Ⓓ give

6. Fill in the _____ under the word.
    I wonder what it is like to go up in _____ .
    - Ⓐ dot
    - Ⓑ mountains
    - Ⓒ box
    - Ⓓ space

GO ON ⇨

Unit 2 Pretest, page 2   Your score: _____

7. Vanessa loves to watch bubbles _____ in the air. We built a beautiful _____ for the parade.
- Ⓐ float
- Ⓑ wagon
- Ⓒ soar
- Ⓓ stand

8. We're getting a new _____ in our kitchen. A cork does not _____ in water.
- Ⓐ table
- Ⓑ light
- Ⓒ sink
- Ⓓ door

Lesson 6: Using Context Clues

Directions Darken the circle by the word that best fits each sentence in the paragraphs below.

9. Were you able to _____ her name in the phone book? Which word means *to find*?
- Ⓐ locate
- Ⓑ print
- Ⓒ read
- Ⓓ draw

10. You need a _____ to steer a canoe on the lake. Which word means *a kind of stick to use with a canoe*?
- Ⓐ bat
- Ⓑ rod
- Ⓒ paddle
- Ⓓ basket

11. Long ago, Native Americans lived in houses made of animal _____ . The houses were called *tepees*.
- Ⓐ plastic
- Ⓑ straw
- Ⓒ bricks
- Ⓓ skins

12. The women in the tribe made dyes and _____ pictures of the Sun, Moon, and stars on their tepees.
- Ⓐ trained
- Ⓑ trimmed
- Ⓒ painted
- Ⓓ pasted

Unit 3 Pretest

⏱ **You have 20 minutes to complete the Unit 3 test.**

Lesson 7: Arranging Sentences in Correct Order

Directions Darken the circle by the sentence that should come <u>first</u> in each of the following groups of sentences.

1. Ⓐ The potatoes were ready to be harvested from the ground.
   Ⓑ The machine stuck its iron fingers down under the potato plants.
   Ⓒ They used the new potato digger.
   Ⓓ It lifted out a clump of dirt and potatoes.

2. Ⓐ For this reason, cities lay underground pipes for their water supply.
   Ⓑ In the city, it would not be possible to get enough water this way.
   Ⓒ The pipes can carry the water as far as 100 miles.
   Ⓓ In the country, people get water from wells and springs.

Directions Darken the circle by the sentence that should come <u>last</u> in each of the following groups of sentences.

3. Ⓐ No one lives in these rooms.
   Ⓑ The President of the U.S. lives and works in the White House.
   Ⓒ Many of the rooms in the White House are used for government business.
   Ⓓ Some of the rooms are offices for the President's staff.

4. Ⓐ She represented hope.
   Ⓑ It was the Statue of Liberty.
   Ⓒ In 1886 the people of France gave the United States a very special gift.

   Ⓓ Today, more than one hundred years later, Miss Liberty is still a symbol of freedom to the world.

GO ON ⇨

Unit 3 Pretest, page 2

Lesson 8: Choosing Titles

Directions Darken the circle by the best title for each paragraph.

5. We had been waiting on the sidewalk for a long time. Suddenly we heard a band playing. Many colorful floats came behind the band. All of the people on the floats waved to the crowd.

Ⓐ Watching a Parade
Ⓑ Waiting on the Sidewalk
Ⓒ Waving to the Crowd
Ⓓ Floating Down the Avenue

6. The loaves in pans move on a special belt to the steam box. As the pans go slowly through the steam box, the dough gets lighter. When the loaves are ready to be baked, they go to the oven. Bread is taken from the oven when it has baked.

Ⓐ The Steam Box
Ⓑ Making Dough Lighter
Ⓒ Many Loaves of Bread
Ⓓ How Bread Is Baked

Lessons 9–11: Reading Stories and Poems

Directions Darken the circle by the answer that best completes each sentence or answers each question.

Dandelion Seeds

Dandelion seeds, dandelion seeds
Fly away, fly
Your soft, white hair will lift you
    so high
The wind will whirl you and
    twirl you
And spin you around
Then gently, so gently,
    you'll fall
    to the ground.

7. What will make the dandelion seeds fly?

Ⓐ the wind
Ⓑ the ground
Ⓒ spinning around
Ⓓ twirling

8. Where will the dandelion seeds fall?

Ⓐ to the ground
Ⓑ in the water
Ⓒ on a hill
Ⓓ on a cloud

GO ON ⇨

Unit 3 Pretest, page 3   Your score: _____

Ava and Sam the Donkey

Ava lived in the mountains with her family and a donkey named Sam. Ava and Sam went everywhere together. Sam was a good mountain climber. He never slipped or fell. Ava was not as good at climbing. She had to be careful where she walked. Where the path was dangerous, Ava would ride on Sam's back. Ava rode the donkey on the path down to the stream. There were fish swimming in the stream. Ava and the donkey splashed in the cool, clear water. Later when they returned home, Ava gave Sam a pail of food. Then Ava went inside for dinner.

9. What is the best title for this story?
Ⓐ A Girl and Her Donkey
Ⓑ How to Train a Donkey
Ⓒ Fishing in Mountain Streams
Ⓓ Ava Has a Swimming Lesson

10. Where did Ava and Sam live?
Ⓐ on a farm
Ⓑ in the mountains
Ⓒ by the shore
Ⓓ in a small seaside village

11. Why did Ava have to be careful where she walked?
Ⓐ She was very clumsy.
Ⓑ She had no shoes.
Ⓒ She was not good at climbing.
Ⓓ She has been blind since birth.

12. Why do you think Ava rode the donkey to the stream?
Ⓐ because the path was long
Ⓑ because the path was dangerous
Ⓒ because he hurt his foot
Ⓓ because she was a lazy girl

13. Which words best describe the water in the stream?
Ⓐ cool and clear
Ⓑ green and slimy
Ⓒ warm and dirty
Ⓓ warm and clear

14. What was swimming in the stream?
Ⓐ a shark
Ⓑ a magical elephant
Ⓒ some beavers
Ⓓ fish

Name _____ Date _____

Unit 1 Posttest   Your score: _____

⏱ **You have 10 minutes to complete the Unit 1 test.**

Lesson 1: Classifying Words

Directions Darken the circle by the word that <u>does not</u> belong with the other words in the group.

1. Ⓐ pencil
   Ⓑ pen
   Ⓒ marker
   Ⓓ paper

2. Ⓐ teacher
   Ⓑ students
   Ⓒ cats
   Ⓓ books

3. Ⓐ penny
   Ⓑ price
   Ⓒ dime
   Ⓓ quarter

4. Ⓐ finger
   Ⓑ thumb
   Ⓒ nose
   Ⓓ wrist

Lesson 2: Using Synonyms

Directions Darken the circle by the word that has the <u>same</u> or <u>almost the same</u> meaning as the underlined word.

5. <u>mend</u> the shirt
   Ⓐ cut
   Ⓑ repair
   Ⓒ wear
   Ⓓ wash

6. <u>harm</u> yourself
   Ⓐ help
   Ⓑ save
   Ⓒ sure
   Ⓓ hurt

Lesson 3: Finding Antonyms

Directions Darken the circle by the word that means the <u>opposite</u> of the underlined word.

7. <u>easy</u> questions
   Ⓐ simple
   Ⓑ hard
   Ⓒ silly
   Ⓓ funny

8. <u>weak</u> ankle
   Ⓐ broken
   Ⓑ strong
   Ⓒ soft
   Ⓓ happy

STOP

Unit 2 Posttest

⏱ **You have 15 minutes to complete the Unit 2 test.**

Lesson 4: Understanding Words With More Than One Meaning.

Directions Darken the circle by the word that has both underlined meanings.

1. used to shine floors
   comes from a beehive
   - Ⓐ honey
   - Ⓑ soap
   - Ⓒ wax
   - Ⓓ comb

2. the opposite of *heavy*
   the opposite of *dark*
   - Ⓐ weak
   - Ⓑ gray
   - Ⓒ thin
   - Ⓓ light

3. someone who cheers for a
   sports team
   something used to move air
   - Ⓐ wind
   - Ⓑ coach
   - Ⓒ fan
   - Ⓓ root

4. dates grow on this kind of tree
   a part of a hand
   - Ⓐ oak
   - Ⓑ finger
   - Ⓒ palm
   - Ⓓ nail

Lesson 5: Choosing Words With More Than One Meaning

Directions Darken the circle by the word with a meaning that fits both of the sentences.

5. Our team needs to buy
   new _____ .
   Did you see those _____
   flying in the barn?
   - Ⓐ uniforms
   - Ⓑ bats
   - Ⓒ caps
   - Ⓓ flies

6. We put all the gifts in the
   _____ of the car.
   It's interesting to watch an
   elephant use its _____ .
   - Ⓐ back
   - Ⓑ trunk
   - Ⓒ seat
   - Ⓓ tusk

GO ON ⇨

Unit 2 Posttest, page 2 Your score: ____

7. Do you know the _____ answer?

Turn _____ at the corner.

ⓐ back
ⓑ left
ⓒ third
ⓓ right

8. I play drums in the school _____ .

Put a rubber _____ around the papers.

ⓐ chorus
ⓑ band
ⓒ stamp
ⓓ play

Lesson 6: Using Context Clues

Directions Darken the circle by the word that best fits each sentence.

9. The clouds looked _____ and gloomy.

ⓐ grade
ⓑ grain
ⓒ grape
ⓓ gray

10. July is a warm _____ .

ⓐ moon
ⓑ mount
ⓒ month
ⓓ mouth

11. Weather forecasters use many _____ to tell us about the weather.

ⓐ tricks
ⓑ games
ⓒ instruments
ⓓ tiles

12. They can tell how hot or cold it will be. They can tell in which _____ the wind is blowing.

ⓐ house
ⓑ direction
ⓒ window
ⓓ kitchen

Unit 3 Posttest

🕐 **You have 20 minutes to complete the Unit 3 test.**

Lesson 7: Arranging Sentences in Correct Order

Directions   Darken the circle by the sentence that should come <u>first</u> in each of the following groups of sentences.

1.   Ⓐ Each plant is set in its muddy bed by hand.
Ⓑ The farmer is barefoot as he walks in the wet fields.
Ⓒ In Asia rice is grown in large, wet fields.
Ⓓ The rice fields are called paddies.

2.   Ⓐ Next spring their buds will open and grow into leaves.
Ⓑ The bare trees are now ready for winter.
Ⓒ Food is stored in their roots and branches.
Ⓓ The leaves will give us summer shade.

Directions   Darken the circle by the sentence that should come <u>last</u> in each of the following groups of sentences.

3.   Ⓐ Then, he rested his head on the desk.
Ⓑ He covered his mouth with his hand as he yawned.
Ⓒ He leaned back on his chair and stretched his arms.
Ⓓ Manuel was very tired.

4.   Ⓐ He threw something silvery on the river bank.
Ⓑ The bear had caught a fish with his big, hairy paw.
Ⓒ The bear kept his eyes on the water.
Ⓓ Then, quick as a wink, his paw struck the water.

GO ON ⇨

Unit 3 Posttest, page 2

Lesson 8: Choosing Titles

Directions Darken the circle by the best title for each paragraph.

5. In the fall, leaves turn many colors. The reds, yellows, and browns look like a beautiful painting. They look especially beautiful near evergreens.

Ⓐ Beautiful Evergreens
Ⓑ Leaves in Fall
Ⓒ Reds, Yellows, and Browns
Ⓓ Painting Pretty Woods

6. The United States Civil War is sometimes referred to as the battle of the Blue and the Gray. Those were the colors of the uniforms worn by the two armies.

These two armies fought for several years. Finally, the war came to an end when General Lee surrendered to General Grant at Appomattox Courthouse. At last the country was united again.

Ⓐ Wars in History
Ⓑ Pretty Uniforms
Ⓒ The United States Civil War
Ⓓ All About Soldiers

Lessons 9–11: Reading Stories and Poems

Directions Darken the circle by the answer that best completes each sentence or answers each question.

Ready or Not
The sky sends different messages
a chill wind is in the air
Darkness comes so soon

Just a few scarlet leaves hang on
here and there a splash of gold
brightens a dark patch of earth

The mood of the world is serious
   now
People look out at tree skeletons
   and snowdrifts
Waiting for spring.

GO ON ⇨

13

7. Why do the trees look like skeletons?
- Ⓐ They're ready for Halloween.
- Ⓑ Their leaves are gone.
- Ⓒ They have some scarlet leaves.
- Ⓓ Darkness comes so soon.

8. Why does the poet call this poem "Ready or Not"?
- Ⓐ Winter will be here even if you're not ready for it.
- Ⓑ You can play Hide and Go Seek.
- Ⓒ The wind is chilly.
- Ⓓ You have to look at snowdrifts.

Washington, D.C., our nation's capital, is a beautiful city. It has wide avenues and tree-lined streets. Millions of tourists visit the city each year. Some of the buildings that people visit are the Smithsonian Institution, the Supreme Court, the FBI building, the U.S. Mint, and the White House.

The U.S. Capitol is one of the buildings that most tourists visit. Both houses of Congress are in the Capitol. One section of the building is for the House of Representatives. The other section is for the Senate. The rotunda, in the center of the building under the dome, separates the sections.

9. You can tell that the author thinks _____ .
- Ⓐ everyone should visit the FBI building
- Ⓑ Washington, D.C., is a good place to visit
- Ⓒ most tourists like the White House best
- Ⓓ the Supreme Court is a special building

10. The Congress of the United States _____ .
- Ⓐ has many buildings
- Ⓑ works at the White House
- Ⓒ meets in the rotunda
- Ⓓ is made up of two parts

11. A building not listed is the _____ .
- Ⓐ Smithsonian Institution
- Ⓑ White House
- Ⓒ Library of Congress
- Ⓓ U.S. Mint

Name _____ Date _____

UNIT 1: VOCABULARY
Lesson 1: Classifying Words

Directions Darken the circle by the word that <u>does not</u> belong with the other words in the group.

Testing Tips

Read each group of words below.
Think about why three of the words belong in the same group.
Then find the word that does not belong with them.

Sample:
- Ⓐ peanuts
- Ⓑ almonds
- Ⓒ walnuts
- Ⓓ apples

Answer

The correct answer is *D. apples.*
Although all the words stand for things to eat, three of the words are about a certain kind of food—nuts. *Apples* are fruit, so this word doesn't belong with a group of words about nuts.

Now Try These

⏱ **You have 15 minutes.**

1. Ⓐ screwdriver Ⓑ saw
   Ⓒ table Ⓓ hammer

2. Ⓐ orange Ⓑ milk
   Ⓒ water Ⓓ coffee

3. Ⓐ cup Ⓑ oven
   Ⓒ plate Ⓓ dish

4. Ⓐ blue Ⓑ grass
   Ⓒ green Ⓓ black

5. Ⓐ spoon Ⓑ chair
   Ⓒ bed Ⓓ couch

6. Ⓐ dog Ⓑ cat
   Ⓒ robin Ⓓ pig

7. Ⓐ people Ⓑ hand
   Ⓒ arm Ⓓ foot

8. Ⓐ eye Ⓑ knee
   Ⓒ ear Ⓓ nose

9. Ⓐ April Ⓑ Friday
   Ⓒ Monday Ⓓ Thursday

10. Ⓐ inside Ⓑ always
    Ⓒ outside Ⓓ under

GO ON ⇨

Lesson 1, page 2

11. Ⓐ kitten   Ⓑ calf
     Ⓒ puppy   Ⓓ horse

12. Ⓐ street   Ⓑ dirt
     Ⓒ road   Ⓓ path

13. Ⓐ cherry   Ⓑ pear
     Ⓒ steak   Ⓓ peach

14. Ⓐ chocolate   Ⓑ ice cream
     Ⓒ vanilla   Ⓓ strawberry

15. Ⓐ eight   Ⓑ number
     Ⓒ fifty   Ⓓ twenty-three

16. Ⓐ two dollars Ⓑ one quarter
     Ⓒ fifteen cents Ⓓ money

17. Ⓐ sleep   Ⓑ jump
     Ⓒ action   Ⓓ read

18. Ⓐ petal   Ⓑ rose
     Ⓒ tulip   Ⓓ lily

19. Ⓐ hair   Ⓑ socks
     Ⓒ shirt   Ⓓ dress

20. Ⓐ cotton   Ⓑ wood
     Ⓒ silk   Ⓓ wool

21. Ⓐ soccer   Ⓑ hockey
     Ⓒ playground Ⓓ tennis

22. Ⓐ plane   Ⓑ farm
     Ⓒ bus   Ⓓ train

23. Ⓐ song   Ⓑ one
     Ⓒ sixteen Ⓓ fifty

24. Ⓐ cow   Ⓑ horse
     Ⓒ pig   Ⓓ fish

Your time: _____

Number right: _____

On this lesson I did _____ because _____

_____ .

I think it would help me to_____

_____ .

Name _____ Date _____

Lesson 2: Using Synonyms

Directions Darken the circle by the word that has the <u>same</u> or <u>almost the same</u> meaning as the underlined word.

⭐ **Testing Tips**

Think about what the underlined word means.
Try saying each choice in place of the underlined word.
Use the underlined word in phrases of your own.

Sample:

<u>seal</u> the envelope
- Ⓐ close
- Ⓑ mail
- Ⓒ open
- Ⓓ receive

Answer

The correct answer is *A. close. Seal* means *close.* Although *mail, open,* and *receive* make sense in the phrase, only *close* means almost the same as *seal.*

Now Try These

⏱ **You have 12 minutes.**

1. <u>chant</u> a tune
   - Ⓐ speak
   - Ⓑ play
   - Ⓒ remember
   - Ⓓ sing

2. <u>total</u> eclipse
   - Ⓐ add
   - Ⓑ destroy
   - Ⓒ complete
   - Ⓓ sing

3. <u>spiteful</u> person
   - Ⓐ mean
   - Ⓑ kind
   - Ⓒ happy
   - Ⓓ good

4. <u>damp</u> clothes
   - Ⓐ dirty
   - Ⓑ wet
   - Ⓒ clean
   - Ⓓ dry

5. <u>follow</u> directions
   - Ⓐ ignore
   - Ⓑ obey
   - Ⓒ think about
   - Ⓓ misunderstand

6. <u>roam</u> down a path
   - Ⓐ skip
   - Ⓑ wander
   - Ⓒ fall
   - Ⓓ swing

GO ON ⇨

Lesson 2, page 2

7. They want <u>extra</u> milk.
- Ⓐ less
- Ⓑ more
- Ⓒ ice
- Ⓓ warm

8. He <u>appears</u> sad.
- Ⓐ seems
- Ⓑ grows
- Ⓒ remains
- Ⓓ leaves

9. What a fast <u>pace</u>!
- Ⓐ race
- Ⓑ animal
- Ⓒ rate of speed
- Ⓓ car

10. Please <u>connect</u> the dots.
- Ⓐ color
- Ⓑ draw
- Ⓒ turn
- Ⓓ join

11. We must <u>protect</u> the forest.
- Ⓐ explore
- Ⓑ plant
- Ⓒ defend
- Ⓓ sell

12. Look at that large <u>meadow</u> of flowers!
- Ⓐ vase
- Ⓑ field
- Ⓒ garden
- Ⓓ store

13. The birds are <u>migrating</u> south.
- Ⓐ eating
- Ⓑ sleeping
- Ⓒ walking
- Ⓓ moving

14. She told us a <u>brief</u> story.
- Ⓐ short
- Ⓑ sad
- Ⓒ long
- Ⓓ funny

Your time: _____

Number right: _____

On this lesson I did _____ because _____

_____ .

I think it would help me to_____

_____

_____ .

Lesson 3: Finding Antonyms

Directions Darken the circle by the word that means the <u>opposite</u> of the underlined word.

 **Testing Tips**

Say each word.
Compare it to the underlined word.
Which word's meaning is the opposite of the underlined word?

Sample:

the <u>strong</u> boy
Ⓐ small
Ⓑ silly
Ⓒ weak
Ⓓ worried

Answer

The correct answer is *C. weak. Strong* means *powerful. Small, silly,* and *worried* make sense in the phrase, but they don't have the opposite meaning of *strong.* The opposite of *strong* is very little power, or *weak.*

Now Try These

⏱ **You have 12 minutes.**

1. a <u>tall</u> tree
   Ⓐ full
   Ⓑ short
   Ⓒ wide
   Ⓓ round

2. the <u>young</u> woman
   Ⓐ pretty
   Ⓑ thin
   Ⓒ small
   Ⓓ old

3. <u>after</u> dinner
   Ⓐ sooner
   Ⓑ later
   Ⓒ before
   Ⓓ earlier

4. <u>quick</u> as a wink
   Ⓐ slow
   Ⓑ still
   Ⓒ cross
   Ⓓ wise

GO ON ⇨

Lesson 3, page 2

5. <u>cheap</u> toys
- Ⓐ idle
- Ⓑ cheerful
- Ⓒ deep
- Ⓓ expensive

6. <u>polite</u> children
- Ⓐ careless
- Ⓑ rude
- Ⓒ happy
- Ⓓ angry

7. This is a <u>special</u> occasion.
- Ⓐ rare
- Ⓑ ordinary
- Ⓒ serious
- Ⓓ happy

8. Will he <u>arrive</u> late?
- Ⓐ stay
- Ⓑ leave
- Ⓒ sleep
- Ⓓ enter

9. The cupboard is <u>bare</u>.
- Ⓐ clean
- Ⓑ empty
- Ⓒ dirty
- Ⓓ full

10. This magic trick <u>always</u> works.
- Ⓐ often
- Ⓑ never
- Ⓒ soon
- Ⓓ sometimes

11. That rug is <u>soaked</u>!
- Ⓐ wet
- Ⓑ dry
- Ⓒ soiled
- Ⓓ wrinkled

12. That is <u>wonderful</u> news!
- Ⓐ sad
- Ⓑ great
- Ⓒ terrible
- Ⓓ old

Your time: _____

Number right: _____

On this lesson I did _____ because _____

_____ .

I think it would help me to _____

_____

_____ .

UNIT 2: CONTEXT

Lesson 4: Understanding Words With More Than One Meaning

Directions Darken the circle by the word that has both underlined meanings.

⭐ **Testing Tips**

Many words have meanings that depend on the way the words are used.
Read the underlined words carefully.
Think of the one word that has both underlined meanings.

Sample:

<u>you have one when you sit</u>
<u>part of a race</u>

   Ⓐ tie   Ⓑ flag
   Ⓒ lap   Ⓓ tape

Answer

The correct answer is *C. lap.* When we sit, we form a *lap.* A complete turn on a racetrack is called a *lap.*

Now Try These

🕐 **You have 12 minutes.**

1. <u>soccer</u>
   <u>wild animals that are hunted</u>
      Ⓐ toy   Ⓑ game
      Ⓒ jungle Ⓓ sport

2. <u>used to style hair</u>
   <u>on top of a rooster's head</u>
      Ⓐ mousse Ⓑ brush
      Ⓒ comb   Ⓓ feather

3. <u>center of a storm</u>
   <u>what we use to see with</u>
      Ⓐ rain   Ⓑ glass
      Ⓒ thunder Ⓓ eye

4. <u>a kind of snake</u>
   <u>a baby's toy</u>
      Ⓐ cobra   Ⓑ block
      Ⓒ rattle   Ⓓ garter

5. <u>something to sleep in</u>
   <u>a place to grow flowers</u>
      Ⓐ bed   Ⓑ cot
      Ⓒ soil   Ⓓ bag

6. <u>wear it on a finger</u>
   <u>the sound of a bell</u>
      Ⓐ ring   Ⓑ mitten
      Ⓒ buzz   Ⓓ chime

GO ON ⇨

Lesson 4, page 2

7. tell to leave a job
start with matches
Ⓐ fire   Ⓑ hire
Ⓒ scratch   Ⓓ smoke

8. grows on a cornstalk
what we hear with
Ⓐ toe   Ⓑ ear
Ⓒ kernel   Ⓓ drum

9. a tool for cutting wood
observed something
Ⓐ hammer   Ⓑ told
Ⓒ knew   Ⓓ saw

10. it cools the air
someone who roots for a team
Ⓐ wind   Ⓑ coach
Ⓒ fan   Ⓓ rain

11. it's found in a shoe
you have one in your mouth
Ⓐ lace   Ⓑ tongue
Ⓒ tooth   Ⓓ heel

12. used to mail a letter
put your foot down hard
Ⓐ walk   Ⓑ address
Ⓒ dance   Ⓓ stamp

13. the season after winter
a coil made of metal
Ⓐ spring   Ⓑ summer
Ⓒ wire   Ⓓ fall

Your time: _____

Number right: _____

On this lesson I did _____ because _____

_____ .

I think it would help me to _____

_____ .

Lesson 5: Choosing Words With More Than One Meaning

Directions Darken the circle by the word with a meaning that fits both of the sentences.

⚡ Testing Tips

The meanings of some words depend on the context in which they are used. Try each answer choice in both of the sentences.

Some words may fit the meaning of one of the sentences, but only one choice fits the meaning of both sentences.

Sample:

These apples cost 99¢ a _____ .
Next, you _____ the nail into the wood.

Ⓐ ounce
Ⓑ pound
Ⓒ strike
Ⓓ beat

Answer

The correct answer is *B. pound*. A *pound* is a unit of weight equal to 16 ounces. Apples are sold by the *pound*. *Pound* also means "to hit," which fits the meaning of the second sentence.

Now Try These

⏱ **You have 10 minutes.**

1. The crowd let out a _____ when the baseball player hit a home run.
   We took flowers to the hospital to _____ my grandmother.

   Ⓐ give
   Ⓑ roar
   Ⓒ yell
   Ⓓ cheer

2. Do you have any time to _____ ?
   Mom noticed that the _____ tire was losing air.

   Ⓐ waste
   Ⓑ spend
   Ⓒ spare
   Ⓓ new

GO ON ⇨

Lesson 5, page 2

3. Elissa was not _____ at the
meeting because she was out
of town.
What birthday _____ did you
give to your friend?

Ⓐ talking

Ⓑ present

Ⓒ gift

Ⓓ attending

4. He wrote a _____ to pay
for the groceries.
The teacher will _____ your
answers.

Ⓐ check

Ⓑ correct

Ⓒ grade

Ⓓ bill

5. I need to go to the _____ for
some groceries.
Let's _____ these boxes in
the attic.

Ⓐ market

Ⓑ store

Ⓒ place

Ⓓ keep

6. May I use this _____ to
measure that picture frame?
The people of that country are
pleased with the new _____
they elected.

Ⓐ yardstick

Ⓑ king

Ⓒ ruler

Ⓓ president

STOP

Your time: _____

Number right: _____

On this lesson I did ___ _____ because _____

_____ .

I think it would help me to _____

_____ .

Lesson 6: Using Context Clues

Directions Darken the circle by the word that best fits each sentence below.

Testing Tips

Read all the words in each sentence.
Read the choices.
Use the context, all the words in the sentences, to help you decide which word makes sense in each sentence.

Sample:

We get lumber from ___S1___ that are cut down in the woods.

- Ⓐ twigs
- Ⓑ trees
- Ⓒ roots
- Ⓓ flowers

Lumber is used to make ___S2___ and other useful items.

- Ⓐ furniture
- Ⓑ clothes
- Ⓒ branches
- Ⓓ flags

Answer

The correct answer for S1 is
B. trees. The clue words are *cut down in the woods*. We don't usually go to the woods to cut down *twigs, roots,* or *flowers*.
The correct answer for S2 is
A. furniture. Do you know why?

Now Try These

⏱ **You have 12 minutes.**

1. Good basketball players practice _____ the ball every day.
   - Ⓐ chasing
   - Ⓑ hunting
   - Ⓒ shooting
   - Ⓓ jumping

2. Practicing is the way they get to be _____ .
   - Ⓐ singers
   - Ⓑ dancers
   - Ⓒ teachers
   - Ⓓ winners

3. Squirrels _____ from tree to tree searching for food.
   - Ⓐ dart
   - Ⓑ sleep
   - Ⓒ dig
   - Ⓓ trip

4. They _____ the food in the ground for the winter.
   - Ⓐ chew
   - Ⓑ cut
   - Ⓒ lose
   - Ⓓ bury

GO ON ⇨

Lesson 6, page 2

5. We _____ mothers on the second Sunday in May.
   - Ⓐ teach
   - Ⓑ honor
   - Ⓒ bring
   - Ⓓ see

6. Mother's Day is a _____ holiday that is observed in our country.
   - Ⓐ sad
   - Ⓑ silly
   - Ⓒ national
   - Ⓓ colorful

7. Did you read the weather _____ for today?
   - Ⓐ man
   - Ⓑ book
   - Ⓒ series
   - Ⓓ forecast

8. I hope it snows so we can go _____ tomorrow.
   - Ⓐ swimming
   - Ⓑ sailing
   - Ⓒ sledding
   - Ⓓ hiking

9. Sounds can _____ through air and water.
   - Ⓐ shiver
   - Ⓑ travel
   - Ⓒ climb
   - Ⓓ drip

10. _____ happen when a sound bounces back through air because it hits a solid wall.
    - Ⓐ Smiles
    - Ⓑ Stories
    - Ⓒ Movies
    - Ⓓ Echoes

11. People are _____ about the amount of water we waste.
    - Ⓐ concerned
    - Ⓑ happy
    - Ⓒ carefree
    - Ⓓ helpful

12. They are worried about the _____ of water for the future.
    - Ⓐ color
    - Ⓑ taste
    - Ⓒ supply
    - Ⓓ weight

Your time: _____

Number right: _____

On this lesson I did _____ because _____

_____ .

I think it would help me to _____

_____ .

26

Name _____   Date _____

Lesson 7: Arranging Sentences in Correct Order

Directions   Darken the circle by the sentence that should come <u>first</u> in each of the following groups of sentences.

**Testing Tips**

When you read the sentences, look for signal words such as *first, next, later, so,* and *then.*
They will help you decide the correct order for the sentences.

Sample:

Ⓐ Then it is harvest time.

Ⓑ The seeds begin growing as they get sun and water.

Ⓒ At planting time, farmers work long hours to plant seeds.

Ⓓ Several months later, the crops are fully grown.

Answer

The correct answer is *C. At planting time, farmers work long hours to plant seeds.* The other sentences tell what happens after the seeds are planted.

Now Try These

⏱ **You have 15 minutes.**

1. Ⓐ In colonial times, people had to think of ways to entertain themselves at home.

   Ⓑ So, we know that colonial children never watched television.

   Ⓒ They read books, played games, or played musical instruments.

   Ⓓ The kinds of entertainment now were not invented yet.

2. Ⓐ Therefore, people who live in this zone do not need to buy warm clothing.

   Ⓑ It is very hot there.

   Ⓒ The equator is an imaginary line around the Earth.

   Ⓓ Countries near the equator are in the torrid zone.

GO ON ⇨

Lesson 7, page 2

3. Ⓐ As a result, we have many different cultures in our cities.
Ⓑ People have come here from all over the world.
Ⓒ They were looking for a better life.
Ⓓ The United States is a nation of immigrants.

4. Ⓐ He is known as one of America's best poets.
Ⓑ Langston Hughes' poems are enjoyed by many people.
Ⓒ His poems are mostly about ordinary African-American life.
Ⓓ He wrote about his experiences in Harlem.

5. Ⓐ Some people like to go to spas for their vacation.
Ⓑ They like the healthy food served there.
Ⓒ They think the spa program will make them healthy.
Ⓓ They like the exercise training.

6. Ⓐ It shines very brightly.
Ⓑ It is easy to find it in the sky.
Ⓒ It is above the North Pole.
Ⓓ Sailors use the North Star to tell which way is north.

Directions Darken the circle by the sentence that should come <u>last</u> in each of the following groups of sentences.

7. Ⓐ It was used to pick seeds from cotton fiber.
Ⓑ Before his invention, most workers could not clean more than a pound of cotton a day.
Ⓒ Eli Whitney invented the cotton gin.
Ⓓ A large cotton gin could clean as much cotton in one day as ten people could do by hand.

GO ON ⇨

Lesson 7, page 3

8.
- Ⓐ His trip created a sensation.
- Ⓑ It created an interest in airplanes as a way to travel.
- Ⓒ Charles Lindbergh was the first person to fly alone from New York to Paris.
- Ⓓ Today, people fly all around the world.

9.
- Ⓐ Then, they are painted with bright colors.
- Ⓑ Native Americans have unique customs.
- Ⓒ First, the poles are carved like animal heads and faces of people.
- Ⓓ Many Native American tribes make special totem poles for their communities.

10.
- Ⓐ After two long days, the storm was over.
- Ⓑ Then, snow began to fall and the wind grew stronger.
- Ⓒ It started with a strong wind.
- Ⓓ Last year there was a terrible blizzard in New York.

11.
- Ⓐ Sometimes weather forecasters use special balloons to study the weather.
- Ⓑ Then, they take these machines back to the lab.
- Ⓒ They hook machines up to the balloons and send them up to the sky.
- Ⓓ When the balloons pop, the machines fall back to Earth.

Your time: _____

Number right: _____

On this lesson I did _____ because _____

_____ .

I think it would help me to_____

_____ .

Name _____ Date _____

Lesson 8: Choosing Titles

Directions Darken the circle by the best title for each paragraph.

**Testing Tips**

Read all the sentences in the paragraph.
Decide what they have in common.
Choose the best title for each paragraph.

Sample:

Jan read a story about an elf. There was a picture of the elf in the book. The picture showed the elf dressed in a black coat, knee breeches, and a broad-brimmed hat. The elf's face was old and wrinkled. He was searching for something in a strange-looking chest. Jan turned the page quickly to find out what the elf found in the chest.

Ⓐ Reading a Silly Story
Ⓑ What Elves Look Like
Ⓒ A Story About an Elf
Ⓓ Searching for Treasure

Answer

The correct answer is *C. A Story About an Elf.* Each sentence in the paragraph tells about an elf.

Now Try These

⏱ **You have 15 minutes.**

1. In the summer, the sheep are washed in clean water. Then, as soon as the wool is dry, it is sheared off the sheep. The wool from each sheep holds together as a mat. The wool is called fleece. If the wool is cut early in the summer, the sheep can grow new fleece. Then they will be warm in the winter.

Ⓐ How Wool is Cut
Ⓑ Caring for Sheep
Ⓒ Weaving a Mat
Ⓓ Keeping Warm

GO ON ⇨

Lesson 8, page 2

2.   Camels store food and water in the strangest way. They store food in the two humps on their backs. They store water in their two stomachs! When they go on long journeys across the desert, they always have their food and water with them.

(A) Crossing the Desert

(B) The Camel's Hump

(C) Strange Animals

(D) How Camels Store Food and Water

3.   Peter was not having a good day. His team wasn't having a good day, either. They were losing the game. It was the bottom of the ninth inning. His team had two outs, and runners were on second and third base.

Peter stepped up to the plate and waited for the pitch. Thwack! He had just hit a double and was now safe on second base.

The next batter at the plate

struck out. But it didn't matter. Who said this wasn't *Peter's* lucky day?

(A) Ninth Inning Problems

(B) Running Home

(C) An Unhappy Team

(D) A Lucky Day After All

4.   Many people travel to the Black Hills of South Dakota to see a magnificent sight. Carved into the side of Mount Rushmore are the faces of four American Presidents. They are George Washington, Thomas Jefferson, Theodore Roosevelt, and Abraham Lincoln. Each of these carvings stand sixty feet tall and can be seen from sixty miles away.

(A) Presidents on Mount Rushmore

(B) Blasting a Mountainside

(C) Stone Mountain

(D) The Black Hills

GO ON ⇨

Lesson 8, page 3

5. Most beavers live in lodges that are built in pools in small streams and ponds. The lodges are made of sticks and mud. Some of them are several feet  high. A part of the beaver lodge always stays above the water, but the entrance is always covered by water.

Ⓐ A Beaver Lodge
Ⓑ How Beavers Cut Down Trees
Ⓒ Tall Beaver Lodges
Ⓓ Using Sticks and Mud

6. Humans are different from animals in many ways. Animals do not think the way humans do. Humans are able to solve problems. They can also figure out ways to do new things. Animals cannot do this.

Ⓐ The Way Animals Think
Ⓑ How Humans and Animals Differ
Ⓒ Thinking of New Things
Ⓓ Solving Problems

Your time: _____

Number right: _____

On this lesson I did _____ because _____

_____ .

I think it would help me to_____

_____ .

Lesson 9: Reading Stories

Directions   Read the story. Darken the circle by the answer that best completes each sentence or answers each question.

⭐ **Testing Tips**

Look at the questions before you read the story.

After you read the story, read the questions again.

Then read all the answer choices. More than one answer choice may seem correct. Choose the answer that goes best with the story.

Some sentences are wrong because they are not true or are not mentioned in the story.

Check your answers by looking at the story.

Sample:

Benjamin Franklin believed that lightning was the same as electricity. Most people thought that this was a foolish idea. Franklin flew a kite during a storm so he could get electricity from the lightning. He proved his theory was right.

Why did Franklin fly his kite during a storm?
- Ⓐ He was a foolish man.
- Ⓑ He wanted to prove his theory.
- Ⓒ He was a clever man.
- Ⓓ He thought that people were foolish.

Answer

The correct answer is *B. He wanted to prove his theory.* The second sentence in the story says that most people thought his idea was foolish. You can guess that he wanted to prove his theory.

GO ON ⇨

Lesson 9, page 2

Now Try These

🕐 **You have 30 minutes.**

Banana plants are not planted from seeds. New plants grow from small shoots that grow from the side of the mature plants. The new plants grow rapidly. They reach their full height in one year. The blossoms appear when the plants are about nine months old. Each plant has one cluster of flowers from which one bunch of bananas will grow.

It takes about three or four months for the fruit to grow large enough to be cut. Bananas are always cut when they are green. If they are allowed to ripen on the plant, they lose their flavor, and the skin bursts open. After the bunch of bananas is cut, the plant dies and is cut down. Then the new shoots grow up to take the place of the old plant, and the cycle begins again.

1. From this story we know that ____.
   Ⓐ bananas are never cut when they are green
   Ⓑ banana skin always bursts open
   Ⓒ bananas are always cut when they are ripe
   Ⓓ bananas are cut when they are green

2. A good title for this story would be ____.
   Ⓐ Visiting a Banana Plantation
   Ⓑ The Life Cycle of Banana Plants
   Ⓒ How to Eat a Banana
   Ⓓ Bananas are Delicious

GO ON ⇨

Lesson 9, page 3

Just imagine! If big rocks had not been broken into little bits, we would not have any food to eat. That is because all the soil on our Earth — the dirt in which we plant flowers and vegetables and grain — is formed largely from rocks that have been crushed by wind, rain, and storms. Of course many other things are mixed with the ground-up rocks to make rich soil. It took hundreds of thousands of years to make our soil.

Some soil is full of pebbles that are larger than grains of sand. This soil is called gravel. Other soil is sandy. Some other soil, called clay, is made up of bits even smaller than sand. These bits are so small that you can hardly see them.

3. How is sand formed?
- Ⓐ from gravel
- Ⓑ from clay
- Ⓒ from pebbles
- Ⓓ from rocks that have been crushed

4. What do we call pebbles that are larger than grains of sand?
- Ⓐ sandy
- Ⓑ gravel
- Ⓒ rocks
- Ⓓ clay

5. What is clay made of?
- Ⓐ broken rocks
- Ⓑ things mixed with ground-up rock
- Ⓒ bits even smaller than sand
- Ⓓ gravel

6. Why do people want to take care of soil?
- Ⓐ They don't like it when the wind blows.
- Ⓑ It takes hundreds of thousands of years to make soil.
- Ⓒ There is too much gravel.
- Ⓓ They want to make a lot of clay.

GO ON ⇨

Lesson 9, page 4

In the winter, most birds fly south so they can live in warmer climates. Birds have been known to fly nonstop across oceans and seas. These flights may not be reported in the news, but they are quite amazing. Just think about how tiny some of these birds are!

One bird, the arctic tern, nests near the North Pole. When their fledglings are old enough, the arctic terns fly to islands near the South Pole. They cross many oceans and many lands. In fact, they spend about half their lives flying.

Robins and bluebirds don't fly so far. They spend their winters in the middle states. Orioles and tiny hummingbirds fly down to Mexico and Central America.

7. According to the story, it is amazing that _____ .
Ⓐ arctic terns live near the North Pole
Ⓑ robins and bluebirds fly to the middle states
Ⓒ tiny birds can fly nonstop across the ocean
Ⓓ hummingbirds fly down to Mexico

8. Another word for *fledglings* could be _____ .
Ⓐ babies
Ⓑ mothers
Ⓒ fathers
Ⓓ parents

9. From this passage, you can guess that the birds that make the longest flights are _____ .
Ⓐ robins
Ⓑ arctic terns
Ⓒ bluebirds
Ⓓ hummingbirds

10. What is a good title for this story?
Ⓐ Birds That Make Nonstop Ocean Flights
Ⓑ When Birds Fly South
Ⓒ Where Some Birds Spend the Winter
Ⓓ The Arctic Tern's Long Flight

GO ON ⇨

Lesson 9, page 5

Anita was excited! This was the day she had been waiting for. Her brothers had been practicing with her and giving her tips on pitching.

Her little-league coach told her that she was going to be the starting pitcher for the play-off game. She was so nervous that she could hardly eat breakfast. She gulped down her juice and cereal.

"Wish me luck," she said to her parents and brothers as she ran out the door. She wanted to talk to the coach before the rest of the team got on the bus.

Four hours later the team returned. Anita ran all the way home. She could hardly wait to tell her family the news about the game.

11. What position did Anita play for her team?
Ⓐ catcher
Ⓑ shortstop
Ⓒ coach
Ⓓ pitcher

12. How do you know that her brothers wanted her to do well?
Ⓐ They practiced with her.
Ⓑ They wished her luck.
Ⓒ They ate breakfast together.
Ⓓ They talked to the coach.

13. What do you think Anita's news was about the game?
Ⓐ The bus got there on time.
Ⓑ The coach let her get on the bus.
Ⓒ They got back in four hours.
Ⓓ Her team won.

14. Which could be a good title for this story?
Ⓐ Anita Eats Breakfast
Ⓑ Anita Pitches a Game
Ⓒ Talking to the Coach
Ⓓ Anita Practices with Her Brothers

GO ON ⇨

Lesson 9, page 6

A banana field in blossom is a beautiful sight to see. It looks like a giant flower garden. The plants sometimes grow to a height of 25 feet! The purple blossoms can be as long as six to nine inches. The great drooping leaves are large and broad. Sometimes the leaves grow to be ten feet long and over two feet wide. They make a wonderful screen that shuts out the sunlight when it is too hot for the plant.

15. To what does the author compare a banana field?
ⓐ purple blossoms
ⓑ drooping leaves
ⓒ a giant flower garden
ⓓ a wonderful screen

16. How do leaves protect the banana plant?
ⓐ They are large and broad.
ⓑ They keep the sun out.
ⓒ They grow to be ten feet long.
ⓓ They have large blossoms.

Your time: _____

Number right: _____

On this lesson I did _____ because _____

_____ .

I think it would help me to_____

_____ .

Name _____   Date _____

Lesson 10: Reading Longer Stories

Directions   Read the story. Darken the circle by the answer that best completes each sentence or answers each question.

Testing Tips

Look at the questions before you read the story.
After you read the story, read the questions again.
Then read all the answer choices. More than one answer choice may seem correct. Choose the answer that goes best with the story.
Some sentences are wrong because they are not true or are not mentioned in the story.
Check your answers by looking back at the story.

Now Try These

You have 30 minutes.

Who is Mae Jemison?

Mae C. Jemison grew up in Chicago, Illinois. Even as a young girl she dreamed of one day becoming an astronaut. She worked hard in school and earned excellent grades.

Mae's extraordinary efforts in grade school and high school gave her the opportunity to go to Stanford University in California. It was there that she received a degree in engineering. Next, Mae enrolled in Cornell University Medical College in New York City. She received a medical degree at this college.

Her dream of becoming an astronaut came true in 1987, when she was accepted in the astronaut program. In 1992, when Jemison was 35 years old, she became the first African-American female to go into space.

1. What was Mae C. Jemison's lifelong dream?
    Ⓐ to become an astronaut
    Ⓑ to become an engineer
    Ⓒ to become a doctor
    Ⓓ to become a teacher

2. Where did Mae study engineering?
    Ⓐ in grade school
    Ⓑ at Cornell University
    Ⓒ in high school
    Ⓓ at Stanford University

GO ON ⇨

Lesson 10, page 2

How to Make a Clay Pot

With practice, anyone can make a simple pot from clay. Take a piece of clay the size of an apple and put it on a flat surface. Press and squeeze it until there are no lumps or air bubbles. Then, using both hands, shape the clay into a smooth, round ball.

Now you are ready to begin. Keep the ball in your left hand. With the thumb of your right hand, make an opening in the clay. Press down toward your palm, leaving a half inch of clay at the bottom. This will be the base of your pot. Now keep your thumb inside the pot. Press the clay gently between your thumb and fingers. Turn the pot after each squeeze. This will make the pot thin out evenly. Continue squeezing and turning until the pot is as thin as you want it.

Now the pot must dry. Cover it with plastic so that it won't dry too quickly. After a few days, uncover it. Then wait a few more days. When the pot is completely dry, it is ready to be fired in a special oven called a kiln. After the firing, the pot will keep its shape.

You may want to add color to your pot. In this case, you would put a glaze on the pot and fire it in the kiln a second time.

3. The first thing you should do when making a pot is to ___ .
  Ⓐ press and squeeze out all the lumps and air bubbles from the clay
  Ⓑ cover the clay with plastic
  Ⓒ shape the clay into a ball
  Ⓓ make the base of the pot

4. Why should you turn the pot after each squeeze?
  Ⓐ so the pot won't be too thick in some spots
  Ⓑ so the pot will have a base
  Ⓒ so the pot will keep its shape
  Ⓓ to remove your thumb

GO ON ⇨

Name _____ Date _____

Lesson 10, page 3

Paul in the Woods

Paul and his friends went to explore the woods. As they walked down a path, Paul noticed a large blackberry bush. He decided to pick some berries for a snack.

Just as Paul reached in to pick some berries, he heard a soft "Coo-coo-coo." He listened carefully and started to look around to see if he could find where the sound was coming from. Suddenly a gray bird fell to the ground. It was flopping about. Paul thought that the bird had a broken wing so he stooped to pick up the bird. But it flopped just ahead of him. So Paul followed the bird. When they were far away from the bush, it flew away.

Paul went back to the blackberry bush. He saw two beautiful white eggs in a nest no higher than his head. He didn't touch the eggs, and Paul and his friends decided to look for another blackberry bush.

Later they saw the bird fly back to her nest. They could hear her saying "Coo-coo-coo," as though she was glad her nest had not been disturbed.

5. Paul reached into the bush because he _____ .
Ⓐ saw a bird's nest
Ⓑ wanted to pick blackberries
Ⓒ heard a strange sound
Ⓓ wanted to help the bird

6. From the story you can guess that the mother bird _____ .
Ⓐ was worried about the eggs in her nest
Ⓑ didn't want Paul to pick berries
Ⓒ had a broken wing
Ⓓ wanted to build another nest

7. The mother bird probably _____ .
Ⓐ wanted the berries for herself
Ⓑ pretended that her wing was broken
Ⓒ had been sitting there a long time
Ⓓ couldn't fly very far

8. What would be another good title for this story?
Ⓐ Paul and His Friends
Ⓑ Let's Go Explore
Ⓒ How to Pick Berries
Ⓓ A Clever Bird

GO ON ⇨

Lesson 10, page 4

What Happened at the Zoo?

Hannah used to live in a large city where she had many friends. When her mother got a job in a small town, Hannah was upset. She didn't want to move. She didn't want to leave her friends, especially her best friend, Sylvia. Hannah's mother promised that they would arrange a visit with Sylvia soon.

One day Hannah's mother asked her, "How would you like to go to the zoo on Saturday? I just talked to Mrs. Reyna on the phone. She and Sylvia can meet us there." Hannah was excited. She couldn't think of anything she'd rather do.

The next Saturday was cold and clear. Hannah put on many layers of warm clothing. She had made a book for Sylvia. It told about all the fun things they had done when they lived next door to each other.

When Hannah and her mother drove up to the zoo, they saw Sylvia and her mother waiting at the entrance. Hannah and Sylvia were glad to see each other. They hurried down the path to the monkey house. "Wait for us there," Mrs. Reyna said. But the girls were so busy talking that they didn't even hear her.

The girls watched the gorillas for a while. They had never seen such large apes. Then they ran to the area with lions and tigers.

They bought some food for the elephants and fed them. They spent a long time watching a giraffe and its baby.

When they started getting hungry, they turned around to look for their mothers, but they couldn't find them anywhere. "Uh oh! I think we might be in trouble," Hannah said. Sylvia was worried, too. The girls sat down and tried to think of what to do.

They decided to follow the signs back to the entrance.

When they had walked a long time, they saw their mothers. Their mothers were happy to see them. They had been worried about the girls. "Where have you been? We've been looking everywhere for you!" Hannah's mother said. The girls didn't know what to say. Later Sylvia

GO ON ⇨

Lesson 10, page 5

whispered to Hannah, "Well, I guess we can add another chapter to the book you wrote. We can write about the time we got lost at the zoo."

9. What is a gorilla?
   Ⓐ a type of lion
   Ⓑ a large ape
   Ⓒ a kind of elephant
   Ⓓ a type of fish

10. What is this story mainly about?
    Ⓐ Hannah's move to a small town
    Ⓑ Hannah's mother's new job
    Ⓒ the monkey house
    Ⓓ the girls' day at the zoo

11. Why did Mrs. Reyna tell the girls to wait for their mothers at the monkey house?
    Ⓐ She liked monkeys.
    Ⓑ She did not want the girls to get lost.
    Ⓒ She was cold.
    Ⓓ She was talking to Hannah's mother.

12. Which words in the story show that Hannah and Sylvia were not near their mothers?
    Ⓐ Then they ran to the area…
    Ⓑ …the girls sat down….
    Ⓒ When they had walked a long time…
    Ⓓ …mothers were happy to see them.

GO ON ⇨

Lesson 10, page 6

13. Why were the mothers upset?
Ⓐ They were tired.
Ⓑ They were worried.
Ⓒ They were lost.
Ⓓ They were hungry.

14. What was the weather like on the day the girls visited the zoo?
Ⓐ hot
Ⓑ cold and cloudy
Ⓒ rainy
Ⓓ cold and clear

15. The boxes below show events that happened in the story.

Hannah and Sylvia met at the zoo.		Hannah and Sylvia fed the elephants.
1	2	3

What belongs in the second box?
Ⓐ Hannah and Sylvia watched a giraffe.
Ⓑ Hannah and Sylvia started getting hungry.
Ⓒ Hannah and Sylvia watched the gorillas.
Ⓓ Hannah and Sylvia found their mothers.

Your time: _____

Number right: _____

On this lesson I did _____ because _____

_____ .

I think it would help me to _____

_____ .

UNIT 3: COMPREHENSION
Lesson 11, Reading Poems

Directions   Read the poem. Darken the circle by the answer that best completes each sentence or answers each question.

★ Testing Tips

Look at the questions before you read the poem.
After you read the poem, read the questions again.
Then read all the answer choices. More than one answer may seem correct.
Choose the answer that goes best with the poem.
Some sentences are wrong because they are not true or are not mentioned in the poem.
Check your answers by looking back at the poem.

Now Try These

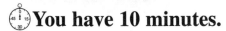**You have 10 minutes.**

Flowers in the Rain
Flowers standing in the rain
heads bent together tightly.
They never, never complain
about the drenching weather.

Soon the Sun will shine and dry
their pretty flower faces.
Then they'll hold their heads
  up high
and shake off all rain's traces.

1. How do the flowers look when it is raining?
   - Ⓐ They stand straight and tall.
   - Ⓑ Their heads are bent over.
   - Ⓒ Their faces are pretty.
   - Ⓓ They smile at the sun.

2. What is another word for *drenching*?
   - Ⓐ bending
   - Ⓑ shaking
   - Ⓒ shining
   - Ⓓ soaking

GO ON ⇨

Lesson 11, page 2

3. What makes the flowers hold their heads high?
- Ⓐ the Sun
- Ⓑ rain's traces
- Ⓒ drenching weather
- Ⓓ pretty flower faces

If I Were Bigger

If I were bigger
I'd climb up that tree
And sit way up on top
Then I'd look down and see
The world all around
Buildings and tiny houses
So close to the ground
I'd see cars and trucks go
    whizzing by
Some go so fast, they almost fly
And I would smile
As I sat up so high
And in a little while
I'd touch the sky.

4. Who is the speaker in this poem?
- Ⓐ a man
- Ⓑ a woman
- Ⓒ a child
- Ⓓ a pet

5. Why would the buildings and houses look tiny?
- Ⓐ The speaker is up very high.
- Ⓑ They are close to the ground.
- Ⓒ They are near the tree.
- Ⓓ The speaker is bigger.

6. Which could be another title for this poem?
- Ⓐ Touching the Sky
- Ⓑ View from a Treetop
- Ⓒ Cars Whiz By
- Ⓓ Climbing Trees

Your time: _____

Number right: _____

On this lesson I did _____ because _____ .

I think it would help me to_____

_____ .

Answer Key

Unit 1 Pretest, page 3
1. B, 2. D, 3. D, 4. A, 5. C, 6. B, 7. C, 8. D

Unit 2 Pretest, pages 4–5
1. C, 2. D, 3. A, 4. D, 5. C, 6. D, 7. A, 8. C,
9. A, 10. C, 11. D, 12. C

Unit 3 Pretest, pages 6–8
1. A, 2. D, 3. A, 4. D, 5. A, 6. D, 7. A, 8. A,
9. A, 10. B, 11. C, 12. B, 13. A, 14. D

Unit 1 Posttest, page 9
1. D, 2. C, 3. B, 4. C, 5. B, 6. D, 7. B, 8. B

Unit 2 Posttest, pages 10–11
1. C, 2. D, 3. C, 4. C, 5. B, 6. B, 7. D, 8. B,
9. D, 10. C, 11. C, 12. B

Unit 3 Posttest, pages 12–14
1. C, 2. B, 3. A, 4. B, 5. B, 6. C, 7. B, 8. A,
9. B, 10. D, 11. C

Lesson 1, pages 15–16
1. C, 2. A, 3. B, 4. B, 5. A, 6. C, 7. A, 8. B,
9. A, 10. B, 11. D, 12. B, 13. C, 14. B, 15. B,
16. D, 17. C, 18. A, 19. A, 20. B, 21. C, 22. B,
23. A, 24. D

Lesson 2, pages 17–18
1. D, 2. C, 3. A, 4. B, 5. B, 6. B, 7. B, 8. A,
9. C, 10. D, 11. C, 12. B, 13. D, 14. A

Lesson 3, pages 19–20
1. B, 2. D, 3. C, 4. A, 5. D, 6. B, 7. B, 8. B,
9. D, 10. B, 11. B, 12. C

Lesson 4, pages 21–22
1. B, 2. C, 3. D, 4. C, 5. A, 6. A, 7. A, 8. B,
9. D, 10. C, 11. B, 12. D, 13. A

Lesson 5, pages 23–24
1. D, 2. C, 3. B, 4. A, 5. B, 6. C

Lesson 6, pages 25–26
1. C, 2. D, 3. A, 4. D, 5. B, 6. C, 7. D, 8. C, 9. B,
10. D, 11. A, 12. C

Lesson 7, pages 27–29
1. A, 2. C, 3. D, 4. B, 5. A, 6. D, 7. B, 8. D,
9. A, 10. A, 11. B

Lesson 8, pages 30–32
1. A, 2. D, 3. D, 4. A, 5. A, 6. B

Lesson 9, pages 33–38
1. D, 2. B, 3. D, 4. B, 5. C, 6. B, 7. C, 8. A,
9. B, 10. C, 11. D, 12. A, 13. D, 14. B,
15. C, 16. B

Lesson 10, pages 39–44
1. A, 2. D, 3. A, 4. A, 5. B, 6. A, 7. B, 8. D,
9. B, 10. D, 11. B, 12. C, 13. B, 14. D, 15. C

Lesson 11, pages 45–46
1. B, 2. D, 3. A, 4. C, 5. A, 6. B

Skills/Achievement Tests Grid
Grade 3

	CAT/5 (Level 13)	CTBS (Book A)	ITBS (Level 9)	MAT/7 (Elem 1)	SAT (9th ed) (Primary 3)	TerraNova (Level 13)	TAAS (Level A)
Vocabulary and Context							
Identifying Synonyms	x	x	x	x	x		x
Identifying Antonyms	x	x		x			
Understanding Word Meaning	x	x	x		x		
Recognizing Words in Context	x	x			x		
Understanding Multiple Meanings	x	x		x	x		
Reading Comprehension							
Identifying Passage Details	x	x	x	x	x		
Determining Sequence of Events	x			x	x	x	x
Understanding Word Meaning from Context	x	x		x	x	x	
Understanding Cause and Effect	x	x	x	x	x	x	x
Understanding Character Traits		x				x	
Identifying Main Idea	x	x	x	x		x	x
Identifying Supporting Details			x			x	x
Predicting Outcomes	x	x		x	x	x	x
Identifying Author's Purpose	x		x	x	x	x	
Drawing Conclusions	x		x	x	x	x	x